The Trout Fishing Song

Written by Jeanne Willis

Illustrated by Clare Elsom

Can I be the look-out?

Can I do the shouting?

4

If you see any trout, you must shout.

I will shout!

"Cast out," said Scout. "Cast out now for a trout."

"The line's out," said Cowboy. "Shout out for that trout."

Cowboys shout loudly but scouts can shout louder.

"Look out!" shouted Scout. "There's a trout! There's a trout!"

This trout that you shout about, has it swum north?
This trout that you shout about, has it swum south?

"That trout," shouted Scout, "is around and about. Around and about with a hook in its mouth!"

"We should cook up that trout," said
Cowboy to Scout. "We should hook it and
cook it and fry it in oil."

I bet you a pound it will spoil and go brown.

Said Scout, "We must hook it and cook it in foil."

"Fry me in oil? It is too hot!" spouted Trout.
"Cook me in foil? I will not stand the heat!"

"Try something different. Try oysters I beg you.
Oysters are many times sweeter to eat."

Alas for our boys, Trout spat the hook out.
Alas for our boys, Trout went on his way.

Were our boys annoyed? No, they both enjoyed oysters.
So sweet and so different they ate them all day!